KEEPING PETS

Mice

Louise and Richard Spilsbury

Heinemann
LIBRARY

www.heinemann.co.uk/library
Visit our website to find out more information about Heinemann Library books.

To order:
☎ Phone 44 (0) 1865 888066
📄 Send a fax to 44 (0) 1865 314091
💻 Visit the Heinemann bookshop at www.heinemann.co.uk/library to browse our catalogue and order online.

First published in Great Britain by
Heinemann Library, Halley Court, Jordan Hill,
Oxford OX2 8EJ, part of Harcourt Education.

Heinemann is a registered trademark of
Harcourt Education Ltd.

© 2006 Harcourt Education Ltd.

Editorial: Andrew Farrow and Stig Vatland
Design: Richard Parker and Q2A Solutions
Picture Research: Maria Joannou and
Virginia Stroud Lewis
Production: Chloe Bloom

Originated by Modern Age Repro
Printed and Bound in China
by South China Printing Company

10 digit ISBN: 0 431 12448 5
13 digit ISBN: 978 0 431 12448 3

10 09 08 07 06
10 9 8 7 6 5 4 3 2 1

**British Library Cataloguing in
Publication Data**
Spilsbury, Louise and Richard
  Mice. – (Keeping pets)
  1. Mice as pets – Juvenile literature
  636.9'353
A full catalogue record for this book is available
from the British Library.

Acknowledgements
The publishers would like to thank the following
for permission to reproduce photographs: Alamy
Images pp. **4**, **7 bottom**, **7 top**; Corbis pp. **8
right**, **19**; Getty Images (Photodisc) p. **42 top**;
NHPA p. **42 bottom**; Harcourt Education Ltd
(Tudor Photography) pp. **5**, **6**, **8 left**, **9**, **10**, **12**,
13, **14**, **15 bottom**, **15 top**, **16**, **17 bottom**,
17 top, **18**, **19 inset**, **20**, **21 bottom**, **21 top**,
22, **23 bottom**, **23 top**, **24**, **25 bottom**, **25
top**, **26**, **27 bottom**, **27 top**, **28**, **29 bottom**,
29 top, **30**, **31**, **32 bottom**, **32 top**, **33**, **34**, **35
left**, **35 right**, **36**, **37**, **38**, **39**, **40**, **41 left**, **41
middle**, **41 right**, **43**, **44 left**, **44 right**, **45
bottom**, **45 top**.

Cover photograph reproduced with permission
of Harcourt Education Ltd (Tudor Photography).

Every effort has been made to contact copyright
holders of any material reproduced in this book.
Any omissions will be rectified in subsequent
printings if notice is given to the publishers.

The paper used to print this book comes from
sustainable resources.

Contents

What is a mouse? .4

Mouse facts 6

Are mice for you? 10

Choosing your mice 12

What do I need? 16

Looking after your mice 22

Handling your mice 30

Health matters 36

Growing old .42

Keeping a record 44

Glossary 46

Further reading 47

Useful addresses 47

Index 48

Any words appearing in the text in bold, **like this**, are explained in the Glossary.

Wha_ is a mous_?

A lot of people around the world are mad about mice! They keep mice as pets because these small, cute, furry animals are friendly, lively, and great fun to watch. Pet mice are different to the wild house mice you see in fields, gardens, or even a house. Pet mice are **domesticated** house mice.

Mouse magic

There are pictures of mice from ancient Egypt. Ancient Egyptians liked to keep mice because they believed that they had magical powers!

People think of wild mice as **pests** because they often feed on farmers' **grain** or steal food from kitchens.

Pet mice in the past

People have been keeping mice as pets for hundreds of years. The earliest record of pet mice was in China over 1,700 years ago. Over time, people bred tamer, more colourful mice. In the 18th century, some wealthy people started to meet and show off their special mice at "fancy mice" clubs. "Fancy" is an old word that means "hobby". Since then, keeping mice has become a hobby for all sorts of people.

When pet mice are awake, they are always on the go and interested in anything they find!

Need to know

- Children cannot buy their own pet mice. When you go to choose mice, you must have an adult with you.
- In many countries, there are laws to protect pets such as mice. You and your family are responsible for looking after them properly. That means you must feed them regularly, make sure they have a comfortable home to live in, and take them to the vet if they are ill.

Mouse facts

Mice are a kind of mammal. Mammals are **warm-blooded**. That means they can warm up or cool down to keep their body at a steady temperature. Mammals give birth to live babies. They also feed their young on milk from their own body. Mice are one of the most common mammals in the world!

Mice are a kind of **rodent**. That means they have sharp front teeth that never stop growing. Other rodents you might have heard of are gerbils, hamsters, and rats. Rodents need to **gnaw** things such as hard foods to keep their front teeth the right length.

Mice are rodents. They have sharp front teeth for gnawing and biting food.

Did you know?

- Mice usually live for one to three years.
- Male mice are called **bucks**.
- Female mice are called **does**.
- Baby mice are called **pups**.
- Adult mice have bodies about 9 centimetres (3.5 inches) long, and have hairless tails almost as long as their bodies – about 8 centimetres (3 inches) long.
- Adult mice weigh about 20 to 40 grams (half to one ounce).

Mice babies

A female mouse can start to have babies from six weeks old. She can have about ten **litters** a year, with about five to seven babies in each litter. That could add up to 70 babies or more a year! In the wild, there are many animals that eat mice, so most young wild mice do not survive for more than a few months.

When they are born, baby mice, or pups, are pink, and have no hair or ears. Their eyes are closed, so they cannot see.

Mice are very good at climbing.

Fun fact

The biggest number of mice pups born in one litter was 32!

Agile movers

House mice are quick on their feet. They can run quite fast and they can swim. Mice are excellent climbers and athletic jumpers. When they run and climb, they use their long tail to help them balance and grip. It is great fun to watch pet mice playing.

Different kinds

There are two types of pet mouse you can have: English fancy mice and American or "common" mice. Most mice you see in pet shops are common mice. Fancy mice are larger, and they have bigger ears and longer tails.

Most common mice have smooth fur, while fancy mice come with a variety of coat types from curly and thick, sleek and shiny, to long-haired or even hairless! Although fancy and common mice look different, they both make good pets and can even live together.

This is a hairless fancy mouse.

Lots of people have pet albino or white mice like this one.

Other types of mouse

You may see other types of mice in pet shops or from mice **breeders**, such as spiny mice and zebra mice. These mice are really only suitable for adults who have a lot of experience in looking after special mice. Most people keep common or fancy mice as pets.

Different colours

The first pet mice were the same colour as wild mice. Mice this colour, called agouti, have dark brown or grey fur flecked with black. Today some pet mice are still agouti, but there are a lot of different colours too, including white, black, black and white, soft grey, and even blue. In fact, there are more than 700 colour and coat varieties!

Mice come in many different colours. This picture shows a black mouse.

Mouse parade

These are some of the different types of mouse you might see.

- Albino – pure white coat, pink eyes, and pale ears.
- Cinnamon – brown fur with dark brown roots, black eyes, and grey ears.
- Argente – reddish-fawn fur with blue-grey roots, pink eyes, and pale ears.
- Red – deep reddish brown with dark brown eyes and ears.

Are mice for you?

Mice make good pets, but there are a lot of things to think about before you choose a pet. You and your family should consider the cost. Even a small pet like a mouse will need food, a cage, litter, and toys, and there will be vet's bills. Here are some of the good and not-so-good points about keeping mice.

If you take the time to get to know your mice, they can become friendly pets.

Mice good points

- Mice are easy to tame and handle.
- They are intelligent and easy to look after.
- Mice are cheaper to keep and feed than many other bigger pets, such as dogs.
- Mice are **nocturnal**, which means they sleep in the daytime and are active when you get home from school.
- Mice make ideal pets if you live in a flat or a small house because they are small.

Mice not-so-good points

- Mice can give off a musky, slightly unpleasant smell, which some people dislike.
- Many mice are shy. It may take a while for them to get used to being handled. Very nervous mice may nip (bite) you.
- Sadly, mice do not live long. Most only live for one or two years.
- If you already have a pet cat, it might be best not to get mice. Cats are one of the main **predators** of mice.

Yes or no?

Have you thought carefully about all the good and bad points of living with a pet mouse or mice? Are you ready to clean out a cage regularly and to give your mice food and water every day, no matter what else you have to do? If the answer to these questions is yes, then it is time to choose your mice!

Choosing your mice

There are a lot of things to think about before you go to choose pet mice, such as how many and what type to get. When you know what type of mouse you want, go with an adult who can help you choose a healthy, happy pet.

How many mice?

In the wild, mice usually live in pairs or small groups and pet mice like to have companions, too. If you are out a lot, it is better to get two mice so they can keep each other company. Two or more females live very happily together. Males can live together if you get them all at the same time when they are young, or if they have always been together from birth.

Top tip

If you get several males, get a big cage so they have plenty of space. This helps to reduce the risk of them fighting each other.

Female mice, or does, live happily in pairs or groups.

Do not put new adult **bucks** together because there is a good chance that they will fight. If your mice start to fight, you must move them into separate cages, away from each other. If you choose to have only one pet mouse, you will need to give it a lot of attention to keep it happy.

Buck or doe?

It is difficult to tell the difference between male and female mice, but a good pet store or **breeder** will keep them in separate cages from a young age. Both bucks and **does** make good pets, but people often choose does because bucks tend to give off a musky smell. The fact that bucks smell also means that their cages may need to be cleaned more often.

Both male and female mice make good pets.

Top tip
The important thing is that you do not put male and female mice together, or they will have babies. It is very difficult to find homes for mice **pups** (babies).

What age?

It is best to get young mice because they will get used to you and your home more easily. Most people get mice that are about five or six weeks old. Mice **pups** should not be taken from their mothers before then.

Where to find a pet mouse

A good place to get mice is from a private **breeder**. You could check with a local vet or at a library to find one. At a private breeder's, you will be able to see if the parents of the mice are healthy. Private breeders also handle their mice a lot, which means they are used to people. Fancy mice will probably only be available from a private breeder.

Many people get mice from pet shops. This is fine as long as you make sure it is a good pet shop. Check that the cages are clean. Make sure **bucks** and **does** are in separate cages and that there are not too many mice crowded into each cage. Ask the pet shop staff questions to check that they know about how to care for mice.

Top tip

If you are getting a doe, check that she has lived separately from bucks from an early age so there is no risk she is pregnant. You do not want the problem of finding homes for a lot of mice pups.

When you get mice, they should be about five to six weeks old, like these.

What to look for

- Pick busy, active mice that have smooth, clean fur and pink, clean skin.
- Check that the eyes, nose, mouth, and bottom are clean and dry. If they are not, it might mean a mouse is ill.
- Ask to handle the mice you might choose, so you can see how tame they are before you bring them home.

Once you have chosen a mouse, you can have fun choosing a name for it. What name would you give this one?

In a pet shop or at a private breeder's, bucks and does should be kept in separate cages like this.

What do I need?

Make sure you have everything your mice will need before bringing them home. The pet shop or **breeder** should give you a special box to bring the mice back in, but you will need to put them into their own cage as soon as you get home.

Choosing a cage

When choosing a mouse cage, think big! It is best to get the largest cage you can afford. For a pair of mice, you should get a cage that is at least 60 centimetres long, 30 centimetres wide and 30 centimetres tall (24x12x12 inches). If you get more than two mice, they will need an even bigger home!

Many people choose cages that have a plastic base with wire sides and top. This kind of cage is easy to clean, lightweight, strong, and fairly cheap to buy. Make sure the solid plastic base is at least 10 cm (4 in) deep, so the mice cannot kick out their flooring material. This also stops cold draughts getting into their sleeping area. Avoid any cages with wire floor or shelves as these hurt mice feet.

Some cages have more than one level and ladders or tunnels for mice to play in.

Top tip

You can buy a plastic and wire cage with several levels or floors, and ladders and tunnels for mice to climb and play in. These can be more difficult to clean, but mice really enjoy them. Or you can buy a tall cage and add your own ramps, ropes, and ladders for mice to play on.

Choosing a tank

Many people keep mice in large aquariums or tanks. These are made of glass or plastic and have a wire cover for a roof. The wire-mesh is important because it lets air through. Glass tanks are quite heavy, so that makes it harder to move and clean them. Plastic is lighter, but the sides may get scratched after a while. If you choose a tank, make sure the lid is always fixed tight so your mice cannot escape.

Some people keep mice in tanks like this or use old fish tanks with wire mesh for a roof.

Make sure the bars on a wire cage are not spaced more than $1/2$ cm (0.2 in) apart, or your mice might squeeze through them and escape.

Top tip

It is best to avoid wooden cages because mice will **gnaw** and damage them. The wood also soaks up **urine** and will smell after a while.

The right spot

It is important to put your mouse cage in the right spot. Mice can get ill if they get too hot or too cold. Put the cage somewhere that is out of cold draughts and away from hot sunlight or radiators. Mice have good hearing and noise can make them nervous, so find a quiet spot for the cage. Avoid putting it in a corridor or playroom, or anywhere busy and noisy. Finally, it is a good idea to put a cage up out of reach of other pets, such as cats. Many people keep mice cages up on a table or wide shelf.

Flooring

Your mice will need something to cover the floor of the cage. Flooring material makes your mice feel more comfortable and helps to soak up their **urine**. You can use wood shavings or pellets made from recycled paper. You can buy both from good pet shops.

Cover the cage floor with the flooring material. Put in a good, thick layer, around 3 centimetres (1.2 inches) deep.

Safety tip

Cedar and pine wood shavings smell nice, but never use them in a mouse cage. Mice can get very sick if they breathe in fumes from these types of wood. Avoid fine sawdust too, because it can irritate a mouse's eyes.

Nesting material

Some mice like to make comfortable nests to sleep in, so your mice will need some material to make themselves a bed. Put some clean straw or shredded paper towels into the cage for this. You can also give them some pieces of paper towel to rip up for themselves.

Do not give your mice newspaper for bedding because the inks in it can be harmful. Do not worry if your mice do not build a nest. They might be happy just to play with the bedding material or burrow under it to nap!

Top tip

All pet mice should have somewhere dark, quiet, and hidden to snooze and rest. It is a good idea to put a bit of plastic pipe, an empty cardboard tissue box, or a small flowerpot into the cage. The mice can use these as a secret hideout or when they need to feel safe.

You can buy shredded paper for bedding or rip up some paper towels yourself.

Mice sleep most of the day, so it is important that they feel warm, safe, and comfortable.

Playtime

When mice wake up in the early evening they get very lively. That means it is playtime! Mice need toys and space to help them get the exercise they need to stay healthy and so they do not get bored. Shops sell a wide range of pet toys, but mice do not need a lot of plastic toys to play with and not all shop toys are suitable. Here are some ideas for good mice toys.

Wheels

Most mice love to run around, so it is a good idea to get an exercise wheel. Choose a wheel carefully. Only buy a solid metal or solid plastic wheel. Never buy wire wheels that have metal rungs or bars, because mice can easily get their tails and feet caught in them. Some cages are sold with wheels in. Others have to be bought separately. Do not be disappointed if your mice do not use the wheel – not all mice like them.

If your mice make a lot of noise on their wheel, you could remove it at night to give you and the mice a break!

Toys around the house

- Cardboard tubes from kitchen paper make great tunnels.
- Cardboard egg cartons are good for climbing, and many mice love to chew on them.
- Stick cardboard boxes and tubes together to make a mouse maze for your mice to run through.
- Lay an open paper bag on its side and watch your mouse play inside.

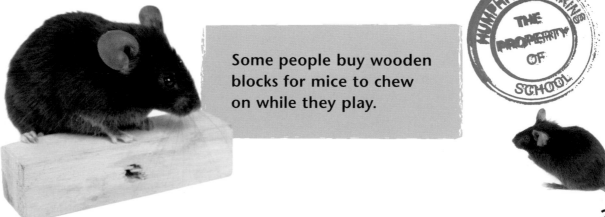

Mice love to climb in, over, up, down, and through things!

Top tip
If you put a branch in the cage, make sure it is safe for your mice to chew on.
It should not have paint or varnish on it as these could make your mice ill.

Climbing

Almost all mice love to climb, so make sure they have some toys they can climb on. You can use ropes, birdcage ladders, branches and twigs, and cardboard tubes. Try tying a long rope in zigzags across the side or the corner of the cage. You can change the rope's position to challenge your mice to find new ways up and down.

Some people buy wooden blocks for mice to chew on while they play.

Looking after your mice

Your pet mice need attention every day. This means giving them fresh food and water, and making sure their cage and toys are clean, and that your mice are healthy.

Mouse mix

Mice may be small, but they have big **appetites**! The main food you give your mice should be mouse mix. You can get this from a good pet shop. There are different types of mouse mix, but they mostly contain **grain**, seeds, pellets, biscuits, and dried vegetables. You can try your mice on different types of mix, but make sure you only buy mouse mix. Do not buy hamster, rat, or other kinds of **rodent** mix for your mice. Not all rodents eat the same things, and a different mix might contain things that could harm your mice.

Mouse mix like this should form the main part of a mouse's diet.

Food facts

- Mice are busy little animals and burn up a lot of energy. Make sure there is always some food in their cage.
- It is best to use a pottery or metal bowl to put the mouse mix in because mice will chew up plastic dishes.
- Instead of using a bowl, you can just sprinkle mouse mix on the cage floor for your mice to find.

Fresh food

You should offer your mice some small pieces of fresh fruit and vegetables every day. Remember to wash fresh food first and only give your mice very small amounts. Try them on some different types to see what they like. Take it slowly though. Mice have small stomachs and too much fresh food can give them **diarrhoea**.

It is also important to remove any fresh food that your mice have not eaten, before it goes **mouldy**. If your mice eat mouldy food, they will get sick.

Choosing fresh food

Peas, broccoli, carrots, parsley, apples, and bananas are good types of fresh food for your pet mice. Never give them cabbage, onion, rhubarb, uncooked potato, or beans as these can give mice stomach ache.

Try different types of fresh food. If a fruit or vegetable makes your mice ill, stop feeding it to them immediately.

Many mice love to nibble on a piece of fresh fruit. Some mice are picky eaters, so do not worry if yours does not like certain types of fresh food.

Clean water

All pets need water every day. Mice are small and they get **dehydrated** very quickly, so you must make sure that they can always get a drink of clean water. It is best to use a glass or plastic water bottle with a metal drinking tube, because mice might knock flooring material into a water dish. They could also knock it over and soak their flooring material. Most water bottles come with a clip that attaches them to the side of the cage. When mice lick the end of the tube, drops of water come out.

Put the bottle at a height your mice can reach easily so they can take a sip of water whenever they want to.

Treats

We know that people should only eat treats once in a while and only in small amounts. Well, it is the same for mice. You can buy special treats from a pet shop to give your mice, but you do not need to. You can get all the treats your mice enjoy from your own kitchen. A lot of mice like a tiny amount of plain biscuit, boiled potato, bread, raisins, cheese, cooked egg, and fish. Never give mice chocolate, corn, sweets, junk food, or peanuts.

Top tips
- Make sure you rinse out the water bottle and fill it up with fresh water again every day.
- When you refill the bottle, make sure the drinking tube is not clogged up.
- Some people add **vitamin drops** to water to help keep their mice healthy, or to give them a boost when they are a bit off-colour.

Top tip
Some people buy mineral and salt blocks for their mice to chew on. Healthy mice don't need these, but some mice like them.

It is okay to give your mice a plain kind of breakfast cereal, but do not offer them any with corn, sugar, chocolate, or peanuts in it.

Feeding time

You can choose when to feed your mice, but it is a nice idea to feed them at the same time each day. If you feed them every evening, tap the cage gently first. If you do this every time, your mice will understand that this sound means it is feeding time. They may run up to the side of the cage ready to take the food from you!

When mice sniff food they are checking to see whether they think it will be good to eat.

Cleaning up

There are some cleaning tasks you need to do every day. You should remove droppings, uneaten food, and dirty bedding every day. Some mice **urinate** in their food bowls, and if yours does this, you will have to clean the food bowl each day too.

Then, once a week you need to clean the cage completely. Ask an adult to help you. To clean a cage properly, you have to throw away all the flooring material and bedding as well as any stale food. Scrub the cage and toys with warm soapy water or water and a safe, pet-friendly **disinfectant**. Then rinse it with clean water and leave it to dry before putting fresh flooring and bedding material in.

Always wash your hands after cleaning the cage or handling your mice.

Top tips

- If you have male mice, you may need to clean the cage twice a week or even more to stop the cage from getting too smelly.
- Mice have an excellent sense of smell. They like it if you put a little of their old bedding back into the clean cage because it smells familiar.

Keeping mice safe

When you clean out their cage, you will need to put your mice somewhere safe. You can buy playpens made of plastic-coated wire panels that clip together so you can place them anywhere. Or simply use a large cardboard box with high sides so that your mice cannot climb out.

Keep your mice nearby while you clean their cage, so you can keep an eye on them.

Holidays

- If you go on holiday, ask someone to take care of your mice while you are away.
- Ask a friend or neighbour who likes mice and does not have a pet cat.
- Leave them clear instructions about what to feed your mice, how to fill the water bottle, and when to clean the cage.
- Leave the phone number of your vet, in case your friend needs some advice while you are away.

If you go away, even just for a weekend, you will need to find someone to care for your mice.

Happy and healthy

Mice spend quite a lot of their time washing and **grooming** themselves. You do not need to bathe or brush them to keep them clean, but it is a good idea to check them regularly to see that they are happy and healthy. For example, are they eating and drinking normally? Are they **alert** and playful, or hunched up and looking miserable?

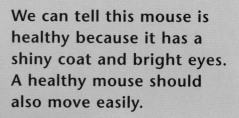

We can tell this mouse is healthy because it has a shiny coat and bright eyes. A healthy mouse should also move easily.

Watch out

Here are some things to look out for when you are watching your mice play.

- How do they move? Do they run and climb easily? If one limps, she may have hurt a leg.
- Are they getting fatter or thinner? Changes in weight can be a sign that all is not well.
- Do they look clean? Do they have runny eyes or a runny nose? Is the area around their tail dirty? These things can be signs of illness.

Daily checks

When you clean out droppings from the cage, check that they look normal. If they are soft, that might mean your mouse has **diarrhoea**. If there are no droppings, it could mean she has **constipation**. When you handle your mice, check that their coats are shiny and flat, not sticking up and patchy. When you stroke a mouse, check that her skin is its usual colour and that there are not any scabs, lumps, or wounds.

To check a mouse's skin, stroke its fur the wrong way along its back and head so you can see the skin.

When you hold your mouse, you will be able to tell if she feels the same as usual. If she feels much lighter or heavier than usual, she might be ill.

Top tip

If you are ever worried that something is wrong with your pet mouse, tell an adult. They can help you decide what to do and whether you need to take her to the vet.

Handling your mice

When you bring your mice home for the first time, you really need to give them time to settle in before you try to handle them. Just put them gently into their new cage and give them a couple of days to get used to the smells and sounds of their new home. Most mice are scared at first, because everything seems strange and dangerous to them. Be patient and your mice will be much happier and friendlier pets.

Getting to know you

After a couple of days, start speaking softly and calmly to your mice so they get to know the sound of your voice. Do not try to pick them up right away. First, let them get used to the smell and feel of your hand. Try gently stroking your mice while they are in their cage. Offer them pieces of food from your hand until they feel safe with you.

Next, try putting your hand in the cage. Keep it still so that your mice can climb on it and sniff your fingers. Do not grab the mouse. Just let him get to know you in his own time. Some mice are more shy than others, so they may take longer to come to you. Do not worry, just try to be patient.

Top tip

Do not try to touch your mice while they are asleep. This can frighten them. If they wake up scared, they may bite you or become scared of you.

Hold your hand still while a mouse takes food from you, so it feels safe.

What if my mouse bites me?

Pet mice very rarely bite people. If they do bite, it is because they are scared. Sometimes they nibble fingers that smell of food, so wash your hands before you play with them.

Tell an adult if you get bitten and make sure they clean the wound carefully. Your mouse should not bite again if you handle it very gently.

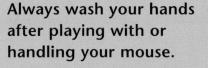

Always wash your hands after playing with or handling your mouse.

Mice time

Once they get to know you, you should spend as much time as you can with your mice. Even when you are busy, try to spend a few minutes with them in the morning and in the evening.

Picking up your mouse

Once your mice know you well, you can try to pick one of them up. First, take off the top of the cage or open the door, and place a hand over the mouse with her nose towards your wrist. Wrap your fingers gently around her body to stop her running away. To pick her up, lift her round the middle with one hand and then cup her in both hands.

This is the only safe way to hold a mouse by its tail.

When you pick up a mouse, hold her gently and do not squeeze her.

Tail care

Never pick your mice up by the tip of the tail or by the middle of the tail because this can hurt them. If you have to catch a mouse that is running into trouble, you can grasp her gently by the base of the tail, which is the part nearest her body. As you lift her, slide your other hand under the mouse to support her body properly. You should never lift a mouse up by its tail alone.

Take it easy

If your mice go to the toilet when you hold them, this may be a sign that they are scared. They may stop doing this if you are much quieter and gentler when you handle them.

From hand to hand

When you have lifted your mouse out of the cage, you can try letting her walk from one hand to the other. Once she has stepped onto one hand, move the other to the front so she can climb onto that one, and so on. Mice are small and very quick, so you will have to be careful. If a mouse tries to jump out of your hand, let her jump onto your lap and then gently pick her up again.

Mice will like to scamper in or on your hands.

Top tips

Mice can be easily hurt, so here are some handling tips.

- Lift your mouse while you are sitting down. If she does squirm and wriggle out of your hands, she does not have far to fall and will simply land in your lap.
- Never lift your mouse up high above the ground. If she falls, she could be injured.

Exploring out of the cage

When your mice are happy to be handled, you can let them out of the cage for exercise every day. First, make sure the space is enclosed and safe. Choose an area where there are no tiny holes or cracks in the wall or floor that they could get into, and where there are no electrical wires or plants that they could chew. Never let them out in a room where a dog or a cat can get in. Move furniture if you think they might get stuck behind it. Use a playpen or pieces of cardboard to enclose the area so they cannot escape.

You can add some new toys to the play area, such as socks and cardboard boxes for them to climb on and explore. Mice love to explore a new spot in your house, but never leave them alone. Be sure to put your mice back in their cage when you leave the room, even for just a minute.

Notice how your mice use their whiskers to sense objects and check out gaps. See how they use their tail for balance as they climb about.

My mouse is very nervous

Like any animals, including people, mice have different personalities. Some are confident and nosy, others are shy or nervous. Nervous mice may bite more, so you may need to wear gloves until they get used to you and stop nipping.

Wearing gloves can give you more confidence when handling a nervous mouse. Try taking them off when he gets more used to being handled.

Your mice will enjoy exploring you.

What if my mouse escapes?

If your mouse escapes, do the following:

- Tell an adult as soon as he goes missing.
- Search the house very carefully. Look everywhere, including under beds, behind boxes, and so on.
- Shut the door to the room and leave food out to tempt him back.
- Do not give up. Sometimes mice can go missing for several days and then you find them again.

Healthy mice have sleek, shiny fur, but sometimes mice get skin problems. A common skin problem is mange, which makes skin dry, flaky, and red, or makes fur drop out. If your mice get mange, you need to take them to the vet. Other skin problems mice may get include lice, mites, or ringworm.

Mites

Mites are tiny, spider-like **insects** that live on some animals, feeding on flakes of old skin. Signs that your mice have mites are that they scratch themselves a lot, they lose patches of fur, and get red patches on their skin. You may be able to see the mites moving in mice fur. They look like very tiny brown specks.

Pet shops sell sprays to get rid of mites. Always ask an adult to help you when you use medicine or chemicals. If your mice have mites, you will also need to clean their toys and cage. Throw away cardboard tubes or any other toys where mites could live. If the spray does not work, see a vet.

You can spray your mice with a special spray if they get mites.

Lice

Sometimes scratching, hair loss, and skin wounds mean your mice have lice, not mites. Lice are tiny, flat, wingless insects that suck blood from a mouse's skin, usually around its neck and body. Lice are larger and easier to spot than mites. Lice can cause **anaemia** or other serious diseases, so you should take your mice to a vet if they have lice.

Ringworm

Ringworm is a more unusual skin problem. It is caused by some kinds of **fungi** that can grow on animal skin. Ringworm will cause round patches on a mouse's skin that look dry, scaly, bumpy, and red, with a clear middle. Mice with ringworm often scratch and they may get bald patches, too. You can treat ringworm with creams and medicine from the vet.

Barbering

If you have two or more male mice, one may try to show he is boss by **gnawing** off bits of another's fur. This is called barbering. Sometimes mice do this to themselves if they are unhappy. People sometimes mistake its effect for ringworm.

You can treat ringworm with special cream from a vet. Ringworm can spread from one mouse to another. If one of your mice gets ringworm, you should put it in a different cage until it gets better.

Cuts and wounds

Sometimes mice get cuts or wounds when they are running about. If this happens, take care of your mouse because cuts can get **infected** very easily. Keep him alone in a clean cage and keep checking the area around the cut. If an **abscess** develops, which looks like a big spot or blister, take your mouse to a vet immediately.
The vet will drain and clean the abscess so it can heal.

If you are ever concerned about your mouse's health, take him to a vet to be checked out.

Teething troubles

Mice have 16 teeth that continue to grow throughout their whole lives, so mice need to do a lot of **gnawing** to prevent their teeth from becoming overgrown. If a mouse's teeth get too long, they can injure his mouth and make it very difficult for him to eat. You will need to take him to the vet to have his teeth clipped back to the correct length.

Lumps and bumps

If you feel a pea-sized bump under or on the skin when you stroke your mouse, take him to a vet. The bump could just be a lump of fatty skin, but it might be a **cancerous tumour**. This can make your mouse very ill, so you need to see a vet about it immediately.

If you stroke and handle your mice every day, you will soon notice if they have any unusual lumps or bumps.

Broken bones

- If your mouse is limping, he has probably fallen or caught his leg and broken a bone. This should heal by itself within a couple of weeks.
- If the bone is not better within two weeks, take the mouse to the vet.
- While it heals, take out any tubes, ladders, or wheels to stop your mouse climbing and making his injury worse.
- Feed your mice bits of bread soaked in milk. The **calcium** in the milk will help the bones to mend.

Breathing troubles

Healthy mice do not make a lot of sounds, so if one of your mice begins to make chattering noises or often breathes noisily or unevenly, take her to a vet. These sounds may mean that your mouse has a **respiratory** or breathing **infection**. Loss of **appetite** and a runny nose can also be signs of a breathing problem. The vet should be able to give you medicine to help. They will advise you on how long you should keep the ill mouse in a separate cage and away from your other mice.

Top tip

Mice sometimes get breathing problems because they have inhaled too much ammonia, a chemical in **urine**. To avoid this, always make sure they have clean bedding.

Encourage your mouse to drink cold water to cool her down if she gets overheated.

Too hot or too cold

Mice are small and they can easily get too hot or too cold. If they get too hot, they breathe rapidly, look unhappy, and may become droopy and weak. Move them somewhere cool and give them plenty of water to drink. If your mice get too cold, they will feel cold to the touch and may become very still and sleepy. Wrap them in a soft flannel and hold them next to your body to warm them up. If these things do not help, go to a vet.

Mice that are sick often try to hide in a corner of their cage.

This mouse shows signs of being quite ill and should be taken to the vet.

Healthy droppings should look like these.

Watch out

- Mice can become seriously ill quite quickly, so watch out for any changes. If any of your mice have any **symptoms** (signs of illness), go to a vet.
- If your mouse sniffles, sneezes, squints, has red-brown tears, a rough coat, and noisy breathing, it may mean she has **pneumonia**.
- If your mouse produces soft runny droppings, she has **diarrhoea**. Stop giving her fresh fruit and vegetables, as this may be the problem. If the diarrhoea does not stop after a day, see a vet. It could be a sign of an infection that a vet will have to deal with.

Growing old

If you are lucky and look after your mice well, they may live for two or even three years. Many mice are healthy and strong for most of their lives, but as they get older most will get some health problems.

Elderly mice sleep a lot. They may not want to play with you very much anymore, but you can still enjoy their company.

Problems of old age

When your mice are old, they will probably not want to play so much and they may sleep a lot more. They also feel the cold more, so make sure older mice are always warm.

Mice are small and if they get sick, they can become seriously ill quite quickly. So keep a watchful eye on them. Older mice are more likely to get **cancerous tumours**, especially behind the legs and on the neck, so check them often. They may also suffer from more breathing problems. If you are worried, see a vet quickly.

When mice are around two years old, they may look thinner, older, and greyer.

A peaceful end

Sadly, mice do not live very long. Some older mice die in their sleep. Near the end of their life, some older mice become ill or they are frequently in pain. Your vet might suggest that you put the mouse to sleep. To do this, the vet gives him an injection that makes him sleepy. His heart stops, and then he dies. He does not feel any pain. This is hard for you, but it might be the best thing for your mouse.

It can help to have a burial place for your pet. Flowers can make it look special.

Marking the end

It is perfectly natural to cry or feel very sad when a pet that you have loved dies. It can help to do some of these things:

- Bury your pet in a special place in the garden and have a ceremony to say a final goodbye to him.
- When you feel sad, talk about it with your friends or family. Most people will understand how you feel.
- Although you will not forget your pet, you will feel better after a while. Then perhaps you could think about getting a new pet.

Keeping a record

Pet mice can be an important part of your life. It is fun to make a scrapbook or record of your furry friends and the things they like to do. You will have fun making it and looking through it, and you will always have it as a reminder of the good times you had with your pet mice.

Words and pictures

You could keep a record of your mouse's progress from the day she arrives home with you. You could add photos of the first time she climbed on your arms or played in her wheel. You could add photos of your mouse playing with her favourite toys, and write about the funny things she does or the games that she plays.

Photos are a great way to remember the good times you have with your pets.

You could keep a record of your mouse's favourite food in your scrapbook.

Mouse manual

You could include information about your mouse's health in your book. For example, the dates and reasons she made any visits to the vet. Or a list of the types of fresh food she likes, and a list of any foods to avoid because they seem to give her stomach ache. This information will also be useful to pass on to a friend if they look after your mouse while you are away.

Useful stuff

You could read other books and find out more information about mice and include this in your scrapbook, too. You may find it useful one day, such as when friends ask for advice about keeping pet mice. You could list addresses of websites that have information about mice and how to care for them. You could also include newspaper or magazine articles and notes about caring for mice.

It can be great fun taking and choosing photos of your mice.

You could add captions and dates to your photos so you can remember when you took them.

Glossary

abscess soft lump that is filled with pus

alert lively and interested in everything

anaemia weakness in the blood leaving an animal weak and tired

appetite desire to eat food

breeder someone who raises a particular kind of animal. A mouse breeder keeps mice so he or she can sell their babies

buck male mouse

calcium kind of protein found in some foods. Animals can use calcium to build or mend bones in their body

cancerous tumour lump caused by cancer. Cancer is a disease that destroys the body's healthy cells

constipation problem caused when an animal's faeces (poo) are very hard, making it difficult for them to go to the toilet

dehydrated when an animal does not have enough water in its body.

diarrhoea runny faeces (poo, or droppings)

disinfectant spray or liquid that destroys germs

doe female mouse

domesticate to tame an animal so that it can live with people

fungi plant-like living things. Some examples of fungi are yeast, mushrooms, and toadstools

gnaw chew or bite

grain seed of a cereal plant such as wheat or barley

groom to clean an animal's fur. Many animals groom themselves

infection illness that makes part of the body fill with pus

insect small animal that has a body made up of three sections (head, chest, and stomach), six legs, and often has two pairs of wings. Flies and wasps are insects

litter a number of baby animals born together

mouldy rotten

nocturnal active at night instead of in the day

pest animal that causes problems for people. Wild mice are pests because they damage farmers' grain stores.

pneumonia illness where the lungs become infected and full of a fluid called pus

predator animal that catches and kills other animals

pup baby mouse

respiratory to do with breathing

rodent animal with strong front teeth that keep growing throughout their lives

symptom sign of an illness

urinate to produce wee

urine wee, a waste liquid that is released by an animal's body

vitamin drops liquid containing vitamins. Vitamins are found in food and animals need certain vitamins to keep them healthy

warm-blooded describes an animal that can warm up or cool down to adapt to its surroundings

Further reading

Mice and Rats (Know Your Pets series), Anna Sproule and Michael Sproule (Hodder Wayland, 1989)

Rats and Mice (My Pet series), Honor Head (Belitha Press Ltd, 2000)

The Wild Side of Pet Mice and Rats, Jo Waters (Raintree, 2005)

Useful addresses

Most countries have organizations and societies that work to protect animals from cruelty and to help people learn how to care for the pets they live with properly.

UK
Royal Society for the Prevention
of Cruelty to Animals (RSPCA)
Wilberforce Way
Southwater
Horsham
West Sussex
RH13 9RS
Tel: 0870 33 35 999
Fax: 0870 75 30 284

Australia
RSPCA Australia Inc.
PO Box 265
Deakin West ACT 2600
Australia
Tel.: 02 6282 8300
Fax: 02 6282 8311

Internet

There are hundreds of pet websites on the Internet. Here are a few that have information for young people.

Visit www.rspca.org.uk the website of the RSPCA (Royal Society for the Prevention of Cruelty to Animals). In Australia, the address is www.rspca.org.au

Go to www.petwebsite.com and there is a section all about mice.

Disclaimer
All the Internet addresses (URLs) given in this book were valid at the time of going to press. However, due to the dynamic nature of the Internet, some addresses may have changed, or sites may have changed or ceased to exist since publication. While the author and Publishers regret any inconvenience this may cause readers, no responsibility for any such changes can be accepted by either the author or the Publishers.

Index

abscesses   38
agouti   9
albino mice   8, 9
anaemia   37

barbering   37
beds and bedding   19,
    26, 40
bones, broken   39
breathing problems
    40, 41, 42
breeders   13, 14, 16
bucks (male mice)   6,
    12, 13, 14, 15, 26, 37
buying your mice   5,
    14–15

cage   12, 16–19
cage cleaning   13,
    26–27
cancerous tumours   39,
    42
China   5
choosing your mice
    12–13
climbing and jumping
    7, 21
coats   8, 9, 28, 29
cold, feeling   18, 40, 42
colours   9
common mice   8
constipation   29
cuts and wounds   38

death   43
dehydration   24
diarrhoea   23, 29, 41
does (female mice)   6,
    7, 12, 13, 14, 15
droppings   29, 41

Egypt, ancient   4
elderly mice   42
escaping   34, 35
euthanasia   43
exercise   20, 34
exercise wheels   20

fancy mice   5, 8, 14
flooring material   18,
    26
food and water   4,
    22–25, 44

glass tanks   17
gnawing   6, 17, 38
grooming   28

hairless mice   8
handling your mice
    11, 30–33, 35
health   15, 18, 21, 23,
    28–29, 36–41, 42, 45
holiday care   27, 45

keeping more than one
    mouse   12–13, 37

lice   37
lifespan   6, 11, 42
litters   7
lumps and bumps   39

mammals   6
mange   36
mineral and salt blocks
    25
mites   36
mouse mix (food)   22

nips and bites   11, 30,
    31, 35
nocturnal activity   11

overheating   18, 40

personalities   35
pests   4
pet shops   13, 14, 16
pets, other   11, 18
playing   7, 16, 20, 44
playpens   27, 34
pluses and minuses of
    mice   10–11
pneumonia   41
predators   7, 11
pups (baby mice)   6, 7,
    13, 14

ringworm   37
rodents   6, 22

scrapbook   44–45
size and weight   6
skin problems   36, 37
smell   11, 13, 26
spiny mice   8

tails   6, 7, 8, 32, 34
teeth   6, 38
teeth, clipping   38
toys   20, 34, 36
treats   24

urine   17, 18, 26, 40

vets   5, 38, 40, 41, 43
vitamin drops   24

water bottles   24
whiskers   34
wild mice   4, 9

zebra mice   8

Titles in the *Keeping Pets* series include:

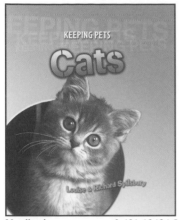

Hardback   0 431 12424 8

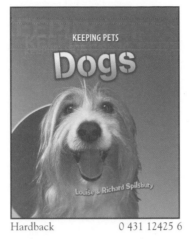

Hardback   0 431 12425 6

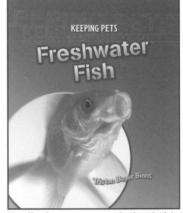

Hardback   0 431 12426 4

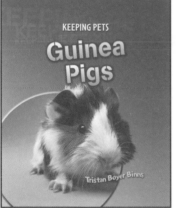

Hardback   0 431 12427 2

Hardback   0 431 12428 0

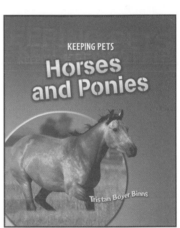

Hardback   0 431 12429 9

Hardback   0 431 12448 5

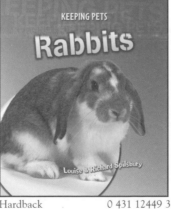

Hardback   0 431 12449 3

Find out about other titles from Heinemann Library on our website www.heinemann.co.uk/library